SHAPE OF A STOMACH

HOW TO BUILD A HUMAN BODY

By Kirsty Holmes

Published in 2021 by Enslow Publishing, LLC
101 W. 23rd Street, Suite 240,
New York, NY 10011

Copyright © 2021 Booklife Publishing
This edition published by arrangement with Booklife Publishing

All rights reserved.

No part of this book may be reproduced by any means without the written permission of the publisher.

Cataloging-in-Publication Data

Names: Holmes, Kirsty.
Title: Shape of a stomach / Kirsty Holmes.
Description: New York : Enslow Publishing, 2021. | Series: How to build a human body | Includes glossary and index.
Identifiers: ISBN 9781978519312 (pbk.) | ISBN 9781978519336 (library bound) | ISBN 9781978519329 (6 pack)
Subjects: LCSH: Stomach--Juvenile literature. | Digestive organs--Juvenile literature. | Human physiology--Juvenile literature.
Classification: LCC QP151.H65 2020 | DDC 612.3'2--dc23

Printed in the United States of America

CPSIA compliance information: Batch #BS20ENS: For further information contact Enslow Publishing, New York, New York at 1-800-542-2595

Photo credits:
Images are courtesy of Shutterstock.com.
With thanks to Getty Images, Thinkstock Photo and iStockphoto.

Ian Struction – gjee. Grid – DistanceO. Front Cover – wonderfulkorea. 4 – doyata. 6–7 – metamorworks, EgudinKa, gritsalak karalak, EgudinKa. 8 – marina_ua. 9 – Visual Generation, Natalyon. 10 – Lemberg Vector studio, Olga Bolbot. 11 – nanmulti, gritsalak karalak, davooda, Meth Mehr, eveleen. 12 – Fir4ik. 13 – lightyear studio. 14 – DandelionFly, Anton Prohorov, archivector, Vadim Almiev. 16 – nilamsari . 17 – Demj, AVIcon. 20 – Noch, AVIcon. 21 – MicroOne, Le_Mon, graphixmania. 22 – Line - design, elegant vector, Amazing vector, Melin Creative, Visual Generation, kosmofish, Cube29, ASAG Studio.
23 – KenshiDesign.

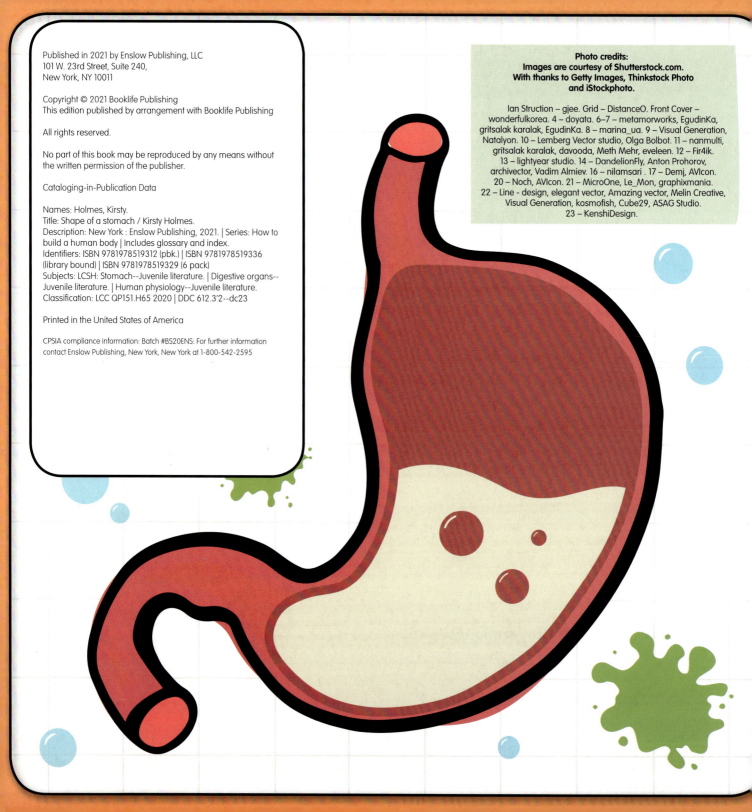

CONTENTS

Page 4	The Body Builders
Page 6	The Human Body
Page 8	The Human Stomach
Page 10	Parts of a Stomach
Page 12	Put It All Together
Page 14	Super Stomachs
Page 16	Troubleshooting
Page 18	Care for Your Stomach: Exercise
Page 20	Care for Your Stomach: Food
Page 22	Activities
Page 24	Glossary and Index

Words that look like this can be found in the glossary on page 24.

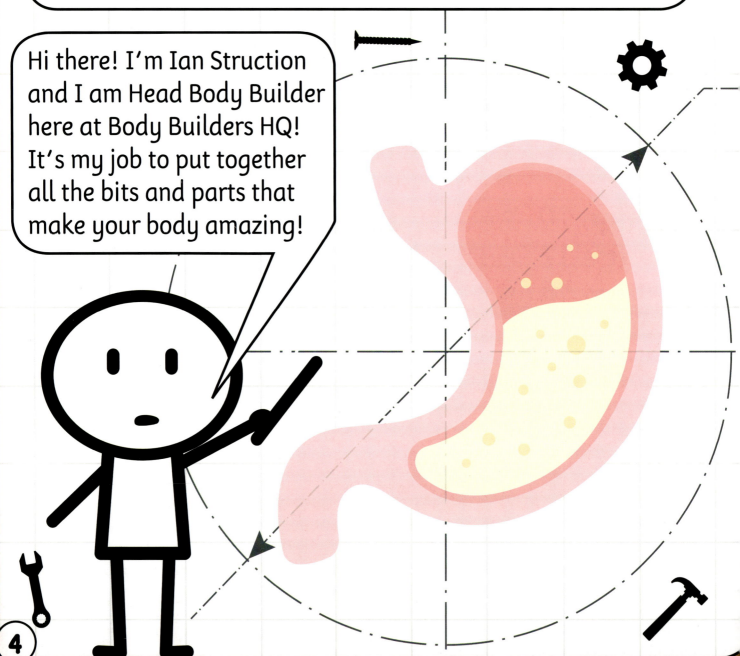

This instruction manual will teach you all about the human stomach. Look out for these signs to help you understand:

Do this

Don't do this

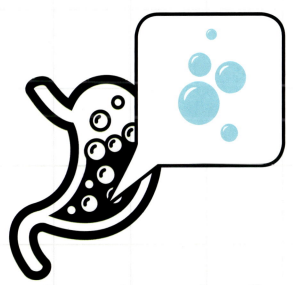

Zoom in on details

More information

THE HUMAN BODY

Your body can do amazing things. Inside you, you have lots of <u>organs</u> that help you breathe, think, eat, and move. Each organ has a special job to do.

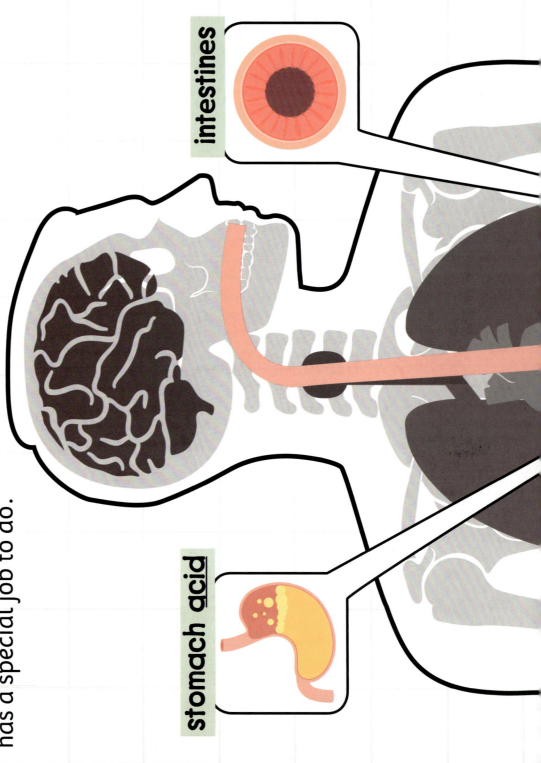

intestines

stomach acid

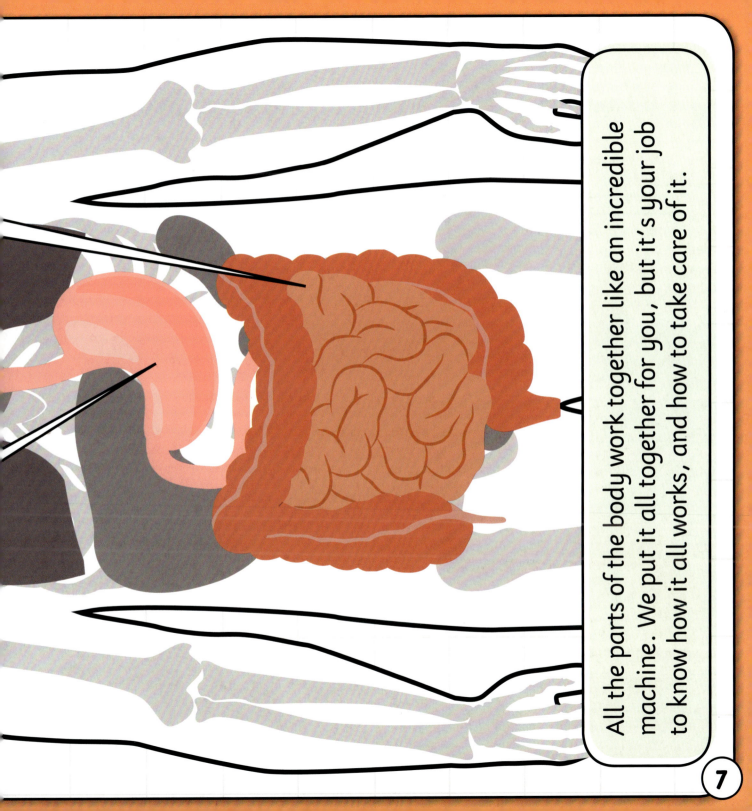

All the parts of the body work together like an incredible machine. We put it all together for you, but it's your job to know how it all works, and how to take care of it.

7

THE HUMAN STOMACH

The stomach is a bag made of <u>muscle</u>. When it is empty, it is about the size of your fist. When you eat, your chewed-up food goes into the stomach to be broken down so it can be <u>digested</u>.

- a bag made of muscles
- can stretch to grow bigger
- makes stomach acid
- breaks down food

Stomach acid helps to kill harmful germs.

The stomach is found in the upper left part of your <u>abdomen</u>. Lower down in the abdomen you have other parts of the digestive system, such as your intestines and other organs.

PARTS OF A STOMACH

For the Body Builders to shape this stomach, we will need:

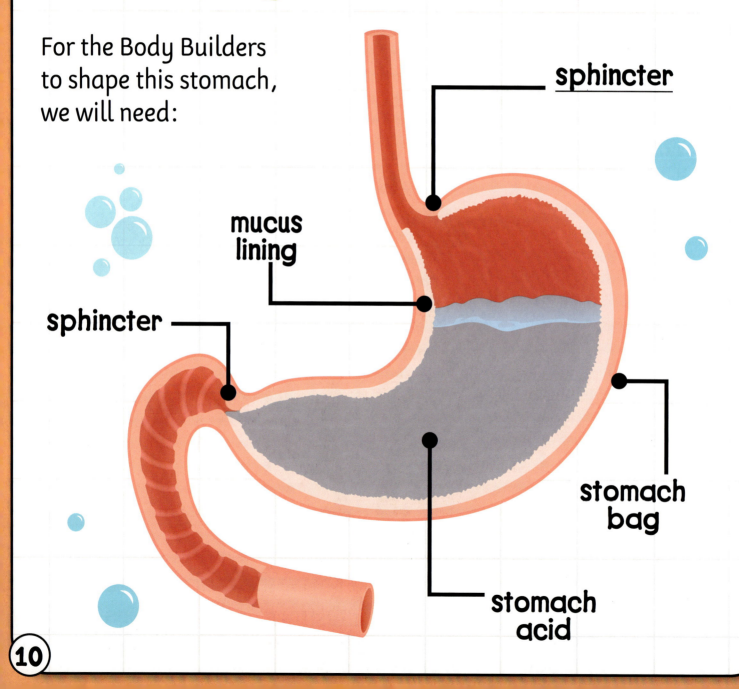

To make the digestive system complete, we will need these things too:

1x esophagus
This tube carries food from the mouth to the stomach.

1x small intestine
20 feet (6 m)

This narrow tube is filled with little fingers called villi that grab <u>nutrients</u> from your food and send them all around the body.

1x large intestine
3 feet (1 m)

This larger tube takes waste away, out of the body.

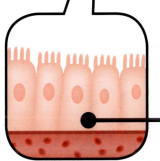

villi

1x rectum
This is where your waste is stored as poop until you go to the bathroom.

1x anus
This small opening is where your waste leaves the body.

PUT IT ALL TOGETHER

When all these tubes are connected, they make up the digestive system. Food is chewed and mashed in the mouth. Then it is broken down more in the stomach.

Your stomach acid breaks down the food into a paste called chyme.

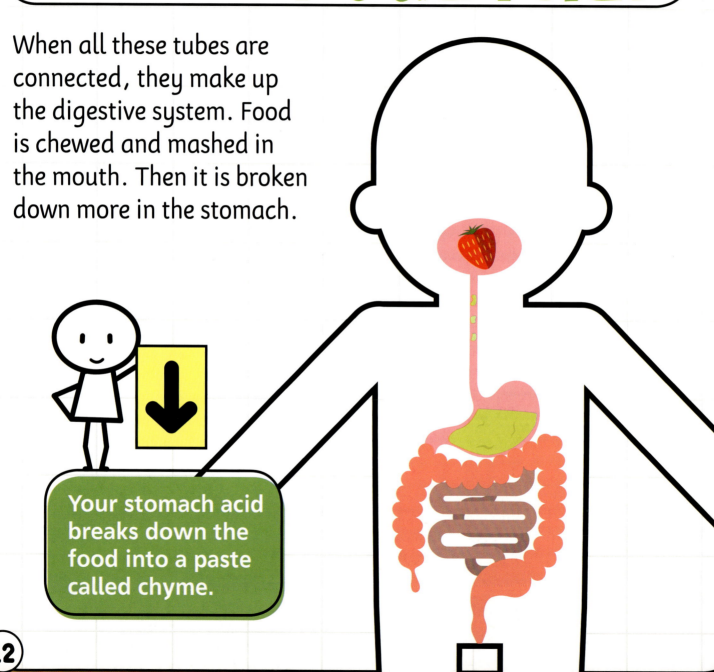

The chyme then passes from the stomach into the intestines, which take in all the nutrients. What is left leaves the body… as poop!

SUPER STOMACHS

Did you know…?

Some animals, such as the seahorse, have no stomach at all.

You should NEVER drink acid—it is very dangerous!

Your stomach lining makes two to three liters of hydrochloric acid every day. This is the same acid that is used in toilet cleaners.

Food stays in the stomach for up to four hours.

When you blush, the lining of your stomach also turns red!

BRRRRP!

When you eat, you swallow air with your food. This air becomes trapped inside you...and the only way to get rid of it is to burp!

TROUBLESHOOTING

A lot of people get a stomach problem called indigestion. This is when the stomach becomes upset and has trouble breaking down food. The main <u>symptoms</u> of indigestion are:

- ✓ pain or a burning feeling in your tummy
- ✓ feeling sick
- ✓ a <u>bloated</u> tummy
- ✓ burping a LOT

Indigestion can be caused by lots of things, such as feeling stressed, or eating lots of fatty or spicy food. You can help indigestion go away, or even keep it from happening, by following our tips here:

Don't eat a lot of greasy food.

Don't eat too quickly.

Find time to relax

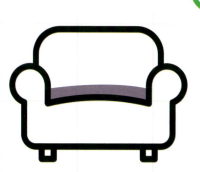

Rest after you've eaten.

CARE FOR YOUR STOMACH: EXERCISE

Being active will help keep your digestive system moving and healthy.

Why not try:

yoga

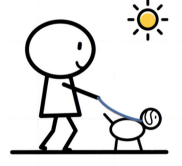
walking the dog

ball games

swimming

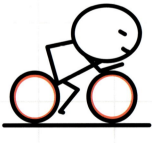
cycling

hiking

gardening

You should aim for 60 minutes of activity each day, and at least three different activities each week. What's your favorite?

dancing

playing on a swing

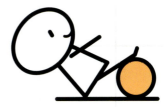
using an exercise ball

Gentle exercise that gets you to twist, bend forward, and move around is the best for your stomach. Dancing to music you like will get you twisting and shaking, and get rid of stress!

CARE FOR YOUR STOMACH: FOOD

Eating foods with plenty of <u>fiber</u> and drinking enough water can help keep your stomach healthy too.

whole grain bread

sunflower seeds

nuts

berries

beans

vegetables

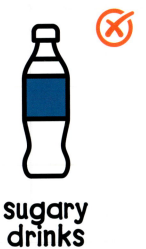 sugary drinks

 fast food

 salt

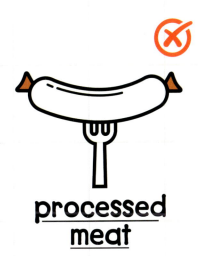 processed meat

 sugar

 lots of citrus fruit

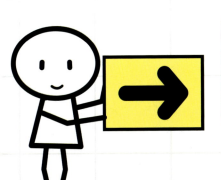

All your organs can benefit from you eating lots of different kinds of fruits, vegetables, nuts, and seeds. Your stomach will thank you!

Bee Breathing

Stress can upset your stomach. Try this exercise to help with any stress you might be feeling. We're going to breathe like a bee! Bzz!

1. **Sit comfortably.**

2. **Breathe in through your nose.**

3. **Breathe out, and hum – hummm mmmm mm...**

4. **Breathe in again and repeat until you feel calm.**

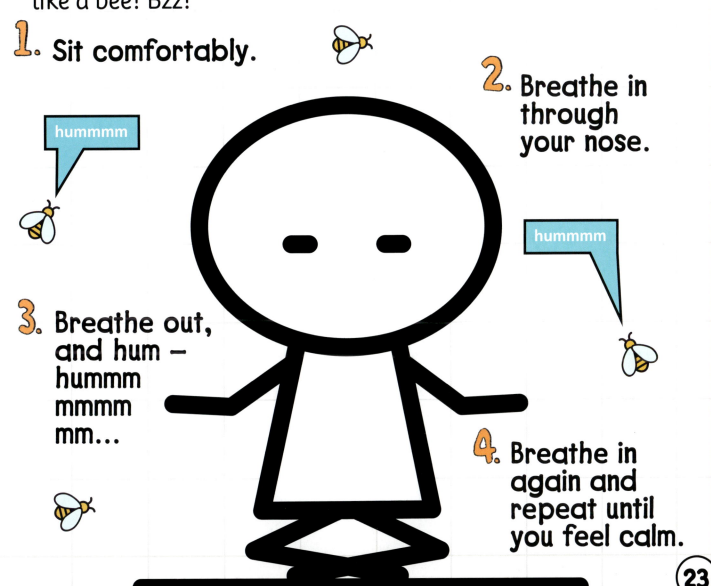

GLOSSARY

abdomen — the part of the body between the hips and the chest
acid — a chemical that can break things down
bloated — swollen; filled with air, food, or water
digested — when the stomach and intestines break down food into nutrients that can be used by the body
fiber — plant matter that cannot be digested; in the body, it helps digestion
muscle — a part of the body that can squeeze together and make something move
nutrients — substances that living things need to grow and stay healthy
organs — parts of a living thing that have specific, important jobs to do to keep the body working properly
processed meat — a meat product that has been changed in some way to make it taste better or last longer
sphincter — a loop of muscle that can open or close a body opening
symptoms — signs of an illness, or the effects of an illness on the body

INDEX

acid 6, 8, 10, 12, 14
chyme 12–13
food 8, 11–12, 15–17, 20–22

indigestion 16–17
intestines 7, 9, 11, 13
nutrients 11, 13

stress 17, 19, 23
waste 11